Feathers In Reverse

Tikum Mbah Azonga

Langaa Research & Publishing CIG
Mankon, Bamenda

Publisher:
Langaa RPCIG
Langaa Research & Publishing Common Initiative Group
P.O. Box 902 Mankon
Bamenda
North West Region
Cameroon
Langaagrp@gmail.com
www.langaa-rpcig.net

Distributed in and outside N. America by African Books Collective
orders@africanbookscollective.com
www.africanbookcollective.com

ISBN: 9956-791-79-2

DISCLAIMER
All views expressed in this publication are those of the author and do
not necessarily reflect the views of Langaa RPCIG.

1. Crisis Meeting

Suddenly, the boss stormed in
Looking drained, flushed out, haggard and jaded
Before we could rise
We were all there
All to the last soul
He ordered us down
"Don`t even bother. I know you all. Band of traitors!
Remain seated, all of you
and take out pens and papers and write!"

Stunned, we slumped into our seats

"Here is the Grail Message
Written just for you.
Prepare the coffins
the time has come
and prepare them now!

As we watched flabbergasted, the tormentor went on:
"Write down everything. Everything!"

"Everything, sir? Even the unanswered questions from Addis
Ababa?" we yelled, fearing for our dear lives.

"Yes, write it all down
That at exactly 3pm local time
The archbishop came this way
He came with no official gear and no company
Alone, all alone
But he carried the Fon`s footstool
That is it!

The meeting is over!"

"But the agenda, sir? What about the agenda?"

Looking surprised, he asked with the air of a Lord
"Agenda, what agenda? I am the agenda
After all, Louis 16th was the State
And the State was Louis XVI!"

With those words, he stormed out of the heavy and sordid
room
And promptly the lights went out
Leaving us to our own devices in the middle of the ocean
"Was he from AES Sonel, or from the capital?", we all
wondered aloud.
But it was too late
The heavy rain had started pelting
And it would go on unabated for two weeks
So where was Mugabe?

2. Those Who Dare To Preach To Us

I will spread it out
I mean, spread it out
With my index finger
It doesn`t matter if it`s too thinly
As long as we square the half mile
We won`t accept any grren notes
Nor the baker`s long loaves
Nor loose euros blowing in the wind
We will tone down any strident calls for blood from DC
We will question and vet
Any petitions to Amnesty and Transparency from Brussels
They`re all talking drums that sound hollow
Because their music is drenched and drowned in sour cheese
droplets
And odd bits and pieces of chicken and chips
And left-overs of last night`s burgers.
We want our own voices to rise up and tower and dwarf
We want our young to grow and step forward
We want our on to show us the way
We want our type to rule and govern
But we reject any go-between
We don`t want godfathers
Just let us be
We turn down all mediators and arbiters
Why should we trust them?
They have betrayed their own people
They carry guns wantonly and shoot randomly like Adolf`s
underlings
They coldbloodedly strap up humans and inject them to
death
They wire them up like some new building and electrocute

them
Their stages and arenas are worse than Hitler`s gas chambers
So who are they to stand and give us lessons?
They`re nothing but opportunists who say one thing and
mean another
They can be all over the place
They can be everwhere
Yet nowhere
They`re brief
Fleeting
Passing
Short-lived
Momentary
Ephemeral
A nine day wonder
So why trust them?

3. The Silence from Rome

The priest is tired
His silk cassock has gone grey
His hands tremble
His mantle no longer fits
His crook looks too heavy for him
Isn`t it time he went?
Shouldn`t he also get a rest?
Or must it only be the pastor?
Leadership is leadership
Unless Rome thinks otherwise.

4. What Colours Mean To Me

(For Marelen)

The girl in white and purple
That's who I am today and tomorrow
That's who I was yesterday
I am my own mistress
I build my own bridges
I trace my own path
I fight my own battles
Life has taught me that the world is inside of us
Not somewhere else
That's why I'm the girl in white and purple
But the colours are the Almighty's, not mine
He alone pulls the strings
And I go at his bidding.

My white and purple

Are not bows without their arrows
They are not the valley lily birds fed yesterday
No, they are a new breed of flower sash from the seamstress
But certainly not a re-enactment of Benson and Hedges.
When we read the Wife of Bath
We do so with due regard for her rattles
That's why my students come here daily without fuss
And my staff work harder than Oscar Wells.
Here at ABCIT where standards are high and far from rubble
We invite all and sundry to come and discover our deep gold
mine
If there is anything tied here, it's certainly strings
That's why with my verse stringer, I'm prepared to go in
hiding.

5. God's Changing Weather
(For Bernadette)

Wao! What a good weather!
Don't you simply love it?
See how meek and lowly
Yet how sweet and charming it is
Yes, it may change
We all know the weather is fickle
But who isn't?
That's life.

For all the exotic readings, I thank the Father
The cumulus, the nimbus, the stratus, they all do it
So does the torrential rain when it rumbles slowly
As a Gemini, I know when the weather is amiss
Like a true child of Babungo, I can measure its full range

So it doesn't matter whether it's a down pour or a trickle
Thank God for the splendid weather and the snow it isn't
After all, without the changes, our Faculty has no real life.

6. Too Big For Charing Cross

I'm not a man to roam
I carry heavy bagpipes
Like the Kilimanjaro poet
Watch my eyebrows
Don't you see them twitch?
So, what more of the wanton birds at Charing Cross?

7. Inches Too Shallow
(For the victim's of Schindler's list)

Some inches were unspeakable
Frankly
Imagine a yarn without fins or spreadsheets
Where on earth would you then begin?
Where?

8. THE WRONG DRINK

I couldn't find the gas pedal
Nor the gradient level
So did I have to sip Ukrainian Cognac?
Just because of that?
What about the charcoal trade?

9. Lone Battle for Christ

I quenched it
Not with holy water
Nor tears for fear
But with God's own spirit
It didn't take long
Although the breath of it was so short
And its Fallopian tubes severed
I did it standing on the Kilimanjaro
Yet, I did it
Don't mind the band master.

We're all damned, profit or no profit
Even if we're offered the best Twin Otter
That's why for ever our offspring will speak from the rear
Especially for those who know Tikrit
And the scapegoat Washington gnawed and gored for so long
The charge is nothing short of tort
It's also nothing short of the leader who once was revered
Forget the dirty bodices and shrunken payroll
What really matters is the last candle no one really lit
And the fact that son is equal to father.

10. A Prayer for Victory
(For Lydienne Blanche)

Give me an example, dear Lord
And a good one, too
For too long I have groped in the dark
Today I want light
I want sunshine
I want your shoulder
I want your hand.

Give me grace, but of your own accord
I don't want to stick like glue
I want to run and worship you like in the park
I want to win with you without a fight
Lord, be my grapevine
Be my solace, my fortress and my giant boulder
So that I too can see the Promised Land.

11. A Certain Point in Time
(For Linda)

I'll think
I'll think and grow rich
Just like Napoleon
Just let the tides ebb away
And the bottom line of Ant & Soc, thicken
That's when we'll even the scores.

I'm not at the brink
That's why I refuse to twitch

9

Instead, I demand brand new dandelions of neon
If you will, that's my way
That's why I must think and ripen
And then get rid of all the pores and sores.

12. My Newest Creation
(For Mayayong)

Every new creation is good
On condition that it doesn't get stuck in the mud
And in the process
Attract odd bits of iron filings
Or some adulterated God's bits of wood
Or even get steeped in sour lime wine.
And that's the plain truth.

Whether I'm called Sandrine or Vera
As long as Spanish is my oyster
And the instructor, this man who makes me laugh
And forever I have this leg in JMC
The world shall continue to spin on its axis
I'm not reinventing the wheel
No, far from it, I'm calling a spade, a spade.

13. The Taunted Lion
(For Agbor Ambang)

So what are you going to do about it?
Let all the chickens loose
Or get them pent up for another month?
Do you think that's fair?
To show a hungry lion meat from the booby
And then abruptly withdraw it?
Is a hungry man not an angry man?

I have come for my search
And I have a torch, just in case
I'm not seeking the heroin
Neither a I seeking the villain
I'm seeking the way to Mamfe
Call me another lotus eater, if you like
I will stand my ground.

14. My Quest for Leadership
(For Kelly)

Why don't I always have what I want
Why is this life this way?
I love my fellow human being
I offer help wherever necessary
But I also want something in return
It's something for something
Not something for nothing
That's what I want.

Yet when I move nearer, they move away

When I go in, they go out
When I go out, the go in
When I call, they giggle
I want my presence to be felt
I want to be present
I want to be seen
I want to be heard
I want to lead
I want to rule the world.

15. Is Man By Nature Good?
(For Ngong Bertrand)

Could people still be this good
Or am I dreaming?
Have heaven's doors and windows
Suddenly flung open and whisked everyone up
With no ticket, no money, no strings?
Why have all the girls` faces brightened up
And all the boys` grips become firmer?
Surely there must be something in the offing.

Cars drive past and I am ticked off as ready food
Amphi 750 is full to the brim and still streaming
All oil paintings I see are like obsolete bows and arrows
Any attempts at changing money simply flop
Science students talk of nothing but concentric circles and
rings
When I attempt to walk up the wrong way, all strung
Multiple hands stop me short of the garner
Today, I wonder how so suddenly man can be so much of an
underling.

16. In The Footsteps Of The Almighty
(For Ronard)

A girl with the fear of the Lord
That's who I am
No more, no less
And I stand my ground
I do so because I know myself

Each time I fall
I pick up myself promptly
And look up to the source of all life
Instantly my spirits return and I take off
The next minute, I`m hearing from him.
Copyright

17. A Field Day For The Vice President
For Akye Nchang

You didn`t look everywhere
Did You?
Did you look among the daffodil beds?Di you look under the
enamel flower pot?
Did you look between the Tilly lanterns?
Did you look among the rejected ballot papers?
Did you even look on the honours list?
That of the newly elected ASJUB officials?

I have a future cut out like Chinaware
I have no fear of that which is new
If you like, I can spin you new threads

13

What I hate is leadership rot
That`s why our new team will always carry lanterns
We do not doubt the value of our peers
So that when the time comes our names shall be on the scroll
That`s why the world, this world, needs presidents.

18. Worms That Snatched Me from Bridget

It wasn`t worms, or was it?
At least not another battalion
For, weren`t we infested and festooned enough?
Did we still have to be inundated, drenched, drowned and
swept away
Like the fish in Pa Muka`s flooded fishponds?
Then what would Dr Oben say in his next peer-reviewed
journal?
After all he was our specialist in fish farming and aquatic
science
This wizard knew all the secrets of the little beast.

Anyway, the house, all of it
Didn`t leak, it just stank
And that was better, if you know what I mean
No amount of perfume from Saudi Arabia
Or dollars from America
Or incense from the Dubai
None of those could change anything. None
So we were all hemmed in, trapped, cornered, caught
I felt rotten as my body touched hers in the darkness
But there was no way I could get onto Facebook
And tell Bridget about it
All about it.

19. A Post Card for Cynthia

I'm inspired each time I see you
It's not your eyes or even your smile
Neither is it your looks
No, it's something else
It's your aura, your body chemistry
You make me feel good
You make me feel high.

With you around me why would I ever want the loo?
Unless we were both sailing down the Nile
And me holding tightly to all my books
Regardless of wherever are all the Earls
Should anyone mention the registry
Then Ill remind them of my hood
And the fact that Cynthia is high.

20. Alone With a Cobweb In Zambia

Did grandpa's cobweb lie
I mean, did it lie through its teeth
Blatantly and unashamedly
While Kamanga was still rising in Lusaka?
And did she notice it at all?
Or was she too overwhelmed by its
multifaceted tentacles and web-construction prowess?

Did the comb-footed spider therefore pry?
And spill the beans as proof of sleuth
Or did it once again, like the Palace Clock of Lusaka

Box itself into a corner and refuse to walk tall?
Then why didn't the rest of us fetch the stilts?
Or were we still waiting for the ill-fated princess?

21. The Bed Wetter

I didn't wet the bed
No, I didn't, I bet you
I just did the pie chart thing
I did it to map out my country
But it came out as Africa
But I did it, remember?
Surely that isn't bed wetting, is it?

I didn't pool it with Ted
I don't believe in tango for two
But I'm wary of the wasp's sting
That's why for the right circumference to comply
One must junket from Luanda to Lusaka to Pretoria and
Accra
Must you be a member?
Well, those who live will know it.

22. The Door the Moderator Snubbed

Will the end lines cross at last
Or will they like the forsaken lap dog
Bark at the wrong target and pop up uninvited for dinner
Letting loose the molten crow bar and cursed smoke-coated
lips
Like another loose canon?

Will the Fon`s whistle blower finally blast
Or will the folded window blinds refuse to twitch
Making Mary's Christmas puddings look like
Half baked cake for the outgoing Moderator?
Surely, that's why our dining lines will never intersect.

23. Where Has My Love Gone?
(For Welle)

Is love real
Or is it just a hollow sham?
Is it papered over cracks
Or yet another act of shoddy contrition?
Why does our church pastor think it`s all sweeping under the
carpet?
What, for God`s sake, is this love?
This demon I can neither touch nor see
Yet daily it blows in the wind
If it be a flower, then which is it?
Is it the rose, the daffodil,the carnation?
The tulip? The anemone? The gladiolus? The Iris or the
rhododendron?
Tell me then; tell me all about it. Will you?

Shall I then never strike this deal
In a world where everything tastes like ham?
Can I blur the writing on its tracks?
Or must I first blow the moderator`s trumpet?
I thought I had hit the treasure trove
And so I quickly wrote to Basel
But look what I have got on the hind
Surely not enough theories or hypotheses to posit
So, when shall I find my long lost love and hold it without
frills?
Does it mean I`ll never dance tango for two?

24. A Ride with God`
(For Jacqueline)

Is that what I want to be
Or is it just a mirage of it?
Am I between a rock and a hard place
Or simply at the end of my tether?
Nay, for a Gemini and a Lesan to boot
I surely deserve better than that
So, tomorrow at midday and unprovoked
I will rise with the falcon
And hedging my bets as best I can
I will with one giant leap but without a single spring
Land on God`s dining table
To him in private will I state my case
And make my point
I`m sure he`ll nod and smile
And lift me back to earth
This time with feet of reinforced steel
No longer molten clay.

25. The Girl with a Heart of Gold
(For Laurantine)

May be I did but did not know I did not
That's life, isn't it?
It isn't about Facebook or yellow nectar or the new gold rush
No, it's the hapless, hungry, stemless sky larks
Who burn their last piece of wood at both ends?
Like the foolish virgins, they walk on their poor heads
And shamelessly dance in the rain on Sundays.

I'm not one ever to blow cold and hot
But as a researcher, I can hypothesize and duly posit
Like the royal broom, I can sweep away any thrush
I know the names of all my brown sharks
And I am an expert at monetary trends
As a Virgo, I can walk on threads
But mind you, I also have my fun days.

26. The Chances I Take
(For Minnette)

I like strangers
Yes, I do
And I make no bones about it
I am prepared to wine and dine with them
Even if it means treading where angels fear to dare
You may say I'm spreading myself out too thinly
So be it
After all, he who ventures nothing, gains nothing
And life is never a bed of roses, anyway.

Do I like debaters?
Of course, I do
Because I firmly believe that to get it you must work for it
Life is not only about Bethlehem
It's also about being fair and paying one's fare
Although I may criticize sorely
I do so in good faith for we can't afford to live life dreamily
Whatever we do must fit
So that for ever we don't lose the silver lining
If we do, then what on earth will ever again hold sway?

27. In Quest Of New Rungs
(For Musi Jane Nanhyigha)

Who am I, really?
A piece of wood flung at the callous wall?
A rotten chunk of meat thrown at the archbishop's dogs?
Or a lone candle stood at the altar by Christ's own successor?
Or am I the next standard bearer to walk up the stairs of the
Kremlin?
Even without going to Delaware? Do you care?
Are you even listening or am I left to my own devices
Stood out in the cold to sing out my voice and lungs?

Why can`t I also move and have my being freely?
Why, like the man of Sisyphus, must I always stall?
Yet my wheels are hampered by no clogs
For I know I belong to the protector
Even if I`ve never lived in Melim
Sometimes I wonder why for once, I can`t also dare
And shout to the world that I too am full of devices
Even if what I need badly are a new set of rungs?

28. Eel on the Heels

Shall we dig in our heels
Or shall we flee?
What does it matter as long as they don`t show glee?
After all, is anyone of us able to come up with an eel?

29. The Ugly Bee

Have they crossed it
Or are the poor souls still thinking about it?
If it`s all been used, then let them tell me
Don`t treat me as if I was the world`s ugliest bee.

30. The Bunch We Are

Are we being hounded
Or simply being rounded
When meat pies become Sunday lunch
Then frankly, we`re nothing but a sorry bunch.

31. Whichever Way

Will the two ever again meet
Or is it just another rotten chunk roasting in the heat?
Even when north and south stand aloof
Why do you quake for sour grapes through the roof?

32. The Unfortunate Jug

Did you say, "River bird?"
Or was it "Cattle herd?"
So what about the red jug?
Or would you rather thrust it at the thug?

33. The Lone Apron

I`m a jaded blue apron
But one with no beefed up icon
And no compressed gas chambers
We were three; now we are one.

34. God`S Chosen One

She is the best
Simply the best, I swear
All with the contours
And the smiles
And the assurances
It`s compatibility at its apex
But it`s not just a union made in God`s house
No, it`s one ordained in God`s bedroom.

So let`s walk abreast
Because that`s where we belong - no wear and tear
Let`s pick a boat and go on a package tour
All of that regardless of the mileage
Regardless of the multiple trances
Even if we are trapped by some entangled latex
Let it be our Garden of Eden
The bride and the bridegroom.

35. My One and Only Orchard Tree
(For Sarah)

You are the person
You are the one and no one else
You are the apple tree
The one I ran into by accident
I mean by pure chance
Yes, you are the one
The one and lone ideal teacher.

You may not be another Pearson
But you are my Oscar Wells
Even if it was all for free
I`d refuse to concede a single dent
Unlike Cyrus Vance
Who grossly tripped before the crown
That`s why with you I`ll always be a sea fairer.

36. A Virgin Gift for the Sultan of Foumban

The founding fathers got it wrong
They got it all wrong
And all of that in the name of political correctness
So let not those of us standing here and now
Claim that our cats were cleaner than theirs
If all we care about is a feline beast
Then what shall we say about
The numerous virgin gifts
Which were all of a sudden
Thrust at the Sultan of Foumban?

37. The Kiss He Planted On Her

I saw him kiss her
He may deny it now, but I saw him do it
He thinks he`s God`s gift to the world
Just let him wait until the soldier ants start biting her.

38. The Missing Cheque Book

I don`t know if it`s here
But I know it was sent
So, check again and have no fear
If you still can`t find it, the caretaker must repent.

39. Bodies That Shame Humanity
(For Funge Diffang)
(An impromptu reaction to the massive group of charred bodies Funge Diffang posted on Facebook today.)

Those bodies aren`t bullet-riddled
They`re charred
They`re lined up
Displayed
Exhibited
Paraded
Arranged, massed up, jumbled up, shuffled, and reshuffled
like a Pack of cards
See how bare they are!
Naked
Unclad
Shamed

Humiliated
Betrayed objects of base value.

Yet they`re human
Even if
Silent
Mute
Uncomplaining
Acquiescent
Oblivious
They too are to someone, somewhere, some how
Husbands
Wives
Fathers
Mothers
Uncles and aunts
Grandparents
Sons and daughters .
Nephews and nieces

So, whose greed is it?
Whose shame?
Whose disgrace ?
Whose humiliation ?
Whose betrayal?
If not ours
We who still live and behold and ponder and contemplate
and wonder
We who still have it all on our laps
Partners in crime
We live to be haunted for ever
By those sordid image
By those macabre images

By those
By this heinous crime
By this dastardly crime
Man`s inhumanity to man
It`s all so disgusting
So repelling
So repugnant
So low
So below-the-belt
So squalid
So foul
So grubby\
So chilly
So horrid
So ghastly
So grisly
So ghoulish
So gruesome
So grisly.

But we`re all guilty
We all have blood dripping
From our pens
From our mouths
From our ears
From our nostrils
From our private parts
From our breath
From our very being
From our space
From our world
From our very being.

When the time comes
The moment of atonement
We shall all give an account
All of all
Singly and collectively
We shall answer questions
Searching questions
Answer for ourselves and for them
Right or wrong
For we are responsible
We are also responsible
This world is one, global
And echo one of us
Is his brother`s keeper.

40. The Mine-Infested Road

It isn`t normal at all
No, forget the packed lunches
For once, pick up your Holy Bible and walk tall
That`s the only way you can avoid the trenches.

41. The Girl From Sierra Leone
 (For Ola During)

I need a man
Wherever I can find one
I need him so that the boss can lift the ban
In that way, I`ll be his Number One.

42. Hold Your Horses

(For Nii K. Bentsi Enshill from whom I learned so much while a Staff Journalist at West Africa Magazine in London, U.K. Nii K. was Deputy Editor and the one in charge of the Franmcophone Desk to which I was assigned. His wide and deep knowledge of French was an asset for me. This was at the   time when the Edirtor was Onyema Ugochukwu and the Editor-in-Chief was Kaye Whiteman)

Let`s not talk about it now
Let`s leave it for the evening before
When you hear the Queen Mother vow
Then wheel out all the pregnant girls to the fore.

43. Awkward One, This

All the swan birds have flown
Taken off before the Fon has sneezed
It has happened before the young have grown
So how shall the lone widows be quizzed?

44. Fee for Zoo Animals

I won`t spare any
All must come down
Down with a bang
So, don`t bet waste your bet.

My club licenses aren`t legion
But my chips are down
So if want an orang outang
We must be ready to pay the fee.

45. So Much Waste Land

Did you use a citation
Or did you just cut and paste?
So when it`s time for confession
What shall you say about all the haste?

46. The Skewed Results

Couldn`t you find the data?
Or was your methodology flawed?
But when it comes to payments pro rata
You wobble as if you had been gored.

47. God`S Only Olive Branch
(For Olive)

Am I strong enough to face the challenges of life?
In other words, do I have my feet firmly on the ground?
Or am I just one of those loose cannons who float and lurk
And in the end, rant and moan and babble?
Am I talking to someone? Are we together?
Or am I a lone voice in the garden of Tibati
In search of greener pastures?
And have I forgotten that today`s my child`s birthday?

I believe in godly harmony, not civil strife
That`s when I`m in my element and on solid ground
Even so, I`m neither, Mandela nor Burke
I don`t dabble in portfolios because I hate tittle-tattle
I `m the compatible Pisces go-getter
And all the princes call me the Beauty Princess from Kribi
I know about all kinds of recipes, although not fixtures
And my secret at all times is one of making hay.

48. Seven Unmarked Posts

What caused it, then? What?
The submerged fjiords or the barren farmlands?
And you stand there and babble and swat
Who do you think will pick up the pieces?

49. The Emir`S Rain

Ask yourself the question again
Is your content larger than life?
And if the Emir were once more to provoke the rain
Who do you think would remmber the stands?

50. Art in All Its Forms

(*To Mwalimu George Ngwane and the rest of us who
were at the AFRICAPHONIE workshop on Art and
Culture Journalism held at the Hotel Residence Carlos
in Buea-Cameroon from the 21st to the 23rd of March
2011. It was three golden days never to be forgotten.*)

This is art, alright
But art with a difference
Just look at the symmetric contours
The concentric and bubbled sounds
The tempered comic relief
The jaded strobe lights
The indented background
It`s not oil on canvass
But you can see the subdued frescoes
Like those of the Sistine Chapel
Call them Velasquez` or Michael Angelo`s if you like
Consider the smoked silver filaments
It`s all picturesque and enameled
It may not be Gothic or baroque
But it`s deep and profound and scintillating
Just watch sky-blue and pacific love birds as they neck
Like the peace plant.

See how their golden vertical and horizontal lines blend
Oh! Don`t they march and merge and fuse and melt?
They thaw out and liquefy into one, single liquid
A slimy and viscous fluid which
Claims its own place in the sun
For how can it miss out on this second Berlin?
Forget about time, distance, speed and velocity
We are talking about architecture
So let`s all together
Gather it all up and hand it to humanity
It belongs to mankind.

Let`s return it to Mother Nature as we received it
Soft
Sleek
Sublime
Innocuous
Majestic
Fresh
New
Pure
Unadulterated
Undefiled
Immaculate
Virgin
Intact.

That`s why here and now, today
As we sit and deliberate on Carlos` throne
We know that South Africa, Ghana and Cameroon are one
United in intention and purpose
It`s several origins, one destination
Several voices, one meaning

Several visions, one object
Several tongues, one expression
Several inspirations, one art
One light
One energy
One source
One soul
One God
The infinite
Nothingness
Zero
Dissipation
Regeneration
Birth
Rebirth.

51. My Girl in the Well
(For my Facebook friends)

Whatever happened to her at the moat
I can`t tell frankly
All I can say is that she missed the boat
Don`t ask me if she did so sadly.

With an aunt whose arms grow weak each day
And a second hand ticket no one wants
How can anyone be surprised she sucks eggs with a spoon of
clay?
That`s why when I think of her I relapse into erotic chants.

Today as the tiny stations fly past like Elstree
And I in First Class am choked by hungry little faces

I wonder whether even she could have remembered the freebie.
If only she knew moats were far off hills, not good races!

52. A Bottle Full Of White Jelly
(For the one and only departmental queen)

He will not be there
When the time comes
Mark my words, the fool will be gone
Gone with the wind
And into the hidden cave
The lake of the Lake Queen
Where dinosaurs revel
On slimy stairs of gold
And stunted jilted girls
Dry out in the sun
Like drunk river birds too lofty to swim
If we prefer to serve as fodder for the cannon
We shall be left behind, stranded and in tears.

53. Alone With the Priest

I don`t like ammunition
Although I love cannons
But if I hear loose cannons
Then I rush to the priest for contrition.

54. The Other Whiff of Grapeshot

I saw the makeshift sandbag whistle past
At an angle too wide to count
At once I picked up my three pinons
And like a wounded lion, shot off to Babylon.

55. Here Comes the Master

Fling out the red carpet
Call out the servants
Wheel out the kids
The master is here.

The men of grace returned him home
Come then and let us make merry
Send a message to Rome
And ask the pope to send back Mary.

56. Thou Art Lord

Oh king of the universe
Let your love flow down in reverse
You are the most high
For those who want to come nigh
You who know our deepest thoughts
Forgive us our torts
You are our fortress, our refuge, our strength
For to you we pay no rent
Stand by us
So that on D-Day we can all step forward without fuss.

57. My Lost Love

Apple of my eye
In nature`s pool you float
When shall I too become a spy?
So that I can lift you like a boat?

My heart cries out with joy
Pretty as you are, you make me pant
Although some may think this a ploy
I know that with you around I`ll never again rant.

58. Standing Betrayed

I have stood out here long enough
Every passing clown has noticed me, poor me
Splashed with pig`s blood
But I alone dry the tears of this nation
Oh! Dream of the forgotten founding fathers!
Was this your wish?

59. Trips Without Tips
(For Gaelle)

The glasses, the teeth and the lips
Those are the trump cards I hold
But perhaps that is only the tip of the iceberg
Which is where our cherished STV comes in
Even so, aren`t we all too slow for the flow?
Have the loose ends at this Carlos Hotel workshop been tied up?
Have all the `T`s been crossed and the `I`s been dotted?
Or have the bosses simply papered over the cracks?

Despite our multiple stilts, I still need some tips
Because as far as I know, I`m firmly back in the fold
Despite the devastating gale from Johannesburg
You are my fresh fish without the fin
My golden compass for the nation despite the foe
Forget about my shouting lipstick so finely lined up
Or my Taurean obstinacy too closely knit to be transported
I move warily enough to avoid the Delegate`s cupid packs.

60. Grandma`S Empty Calabashes

In none of these three calabashes
Has grandma dumped her ashes
If we weep, she dips her index finger
If we creep, she turns into a waxwork figure.

61. Faced With a Weakened People
(For sons and daughters of the Baforchu-Mbu clan)

Why so much sorrow in the oracle`s heart of hearts?
Why do cumulus and nimbus clouds gather momentum?
Why do the hillside palace owls mourn?
Why has the black smoke not fissured out?
Why is our Fon still snoring?

If the young people of the village think tradition is only an art
And thus reduce it to the age-old mbaghalum
Then perhaps they`re living in the shrine room
Ignoring the calls of Maformusong for all to come out
If this goes on, shall we be saved from perishing?

62. Jelly with no Viscuosity

Is there sorrow or joy in the bulwark stars
That peck away at God`s living boars
Or is all the fire in the wolf`s belly
Simply another crude form of petroleum jelly.

63. The Mad Moment

I didn`t hear the window clatter
But I heard the giant bird flap its sodden wings
And the ugly sky bare its rotten fangs
That was when the tides turned.

For someone whose life has all been in rubber
I can`t help thinking of my million slings
And all the stray orang outangs
Put together, they`re like Saddam`s things all churned.

64. Barefooted For the Pope

I own nothing but my bare feet
My tinderboxes and golden cymbals all went
They went with the wind
Now that the pope wants me
To sing and dance waltz for two
What shall I tell the parish priest?

65. Memories of Lusaka

I own no mango boughs
Although I have worked in boroughs
A child of a mangled past
Since the good old days with Chipimo in Lusaka
I hop in and out as I like
And the holy ground at all times
Remains the holy ground.

66. Why Should She Do It?

Yes, why on earth should she do it today?
Did she do it yesterday?
Why should the poor girl auction her body
Only to go to hell feet-bound?
It`s Sunday morning in Las Vegas, you know?

While no one else is held at bay
But everyone hails everything made of clay
All your dirty mind sees are Easter eggs made shoddy
Aren`t you therefore one of those who hound
Ho hound and suck and fondle and throw?

67. The Other Tea Party

Tea and sea may sound alike
But none is like Boston or a bike
So when death becomes the mother of beauty
Time and space become a lasting couple.

68. Paying For Incidentals

The naked books are open
And the glass nobs warm
When the green wings are flown in
And all slovenly requitals become lustful recitals
Won`t we all become muttering landlords?

69. Compass Reading
(For Nasare)

I`ll go no more aroving
I promise you
Even if the sky comes down on my head
And that`s final.

So when you go round beaming
Spare a thought for Jacob`s zoo
Where wrought iron has turned into allowed lead.
If you trust me, buy me a sparkling crystal.

70. One More for the Risen Christ

I though I gave you one
Or am I dreaming?
Why would I, when the swan birds haven`t flown past?
Neither has the minister`s heart beat risen?

What we need most in Christendom is a crown
For God`s sake, not another farthing!
Lest the boss flies the flag at half mast
So let`s rejoice for Christ has risen.

71. A Cheer for Pisces and Taurus
(For Caroline)

Make a path and let others follow
Don`t just stand back and look askance
After all weren`t it for this film launch where angels lie fallow
Why would anyonwe go into a trance?

Life isn`t only Shakespeare`s sonnets all so hollow
No, it`s also an arena full of surprises and a firm stance
A platform where Taurean and Piscean of age frolic and
wallow
Melting into each other and hustling and jostling at the
entrance.

72. A Dinghy for Ndingi
(For Elangwe Ndingi)

Imaginary doing
And imaginary underlings
That`s what I loathe most
But when it comes to candle light
And the wild roars of the deep blue sea
I surely gird my loins aright
And step into the arena.

Don`t we all love hoeing?
Or do you prefer David`s slings?
And those Achirimbi anemones about which you boast?
If you`re not ready for the fight
Then I`ll write to the Holy See
And request another dinghy by right

If you don`t like it, go to Ndjamena.

73. What Being a Delegate Means
(For Saahkem Nancy Ephe)

A girl with a difference
That`s what we all are
Forget Margaret Thatcher and her knighthood
I am also a Baroness
Baroness Saahkem
So let`s all go back to the bank
And count all the dormant butterflies.

Whether you pick the conference or the circumference
The light green lace will never be far
And that`s when nothing counts but brotherhood
For delegates like us who are full of prowess
And who yearn daily to go to Bethlehem
Far from being a question of rank
It`s a matter of who first spots the water lilies.

74. Shows with No Starting Time
(For Ma Stella of Buea)

Do I go to the net
Or do you just want me to play to the gallery?
I`m not a pretender
Neither am I an actress
I don`t paper over the cracks
Neither do I sweep things under the carpet.

You may very well call me your little pet
But don`t send me to Calgary
Even if like Stephen, I`m an iron bender
All I need is a little recess
So that I can mend the stable in the barracks
That`s when all shows will merge to become one puppet.

75. Trousers That Won't Fit
(For Missline)

Happy and unhappy trousers
That's what I wore yesterday
That's what I'm wearing today
And that's what I'll wear tomorrow
After all, why not?
Is life itself not happy and unhappy?

I fret when mankind flounders
And nothing else holds sway
That's why at all cost I shun the fray
As Sagittarius I also feel sorrow
But as the born fighter I can reduce it to naught
Outspoken? You bet! But I'm also snappy.

76. Daddy's One and only Daughter
(For Marion)

Tribute to my late dad
That's what I have to say
And I mean it
I say it from the bottom of my heart
Dad, accept this as my Golden Fleece
My sacred bouquet of flowers
My genuine words of thanksgiving
You deserve it all.

Without you, I wouldn't be clad
And I would never have my day
Even if I was fit
You loved me from the very start
Even when you went to Greece
That was when you brought back the louvers
Today that I am here, all alone and grieving
I know you want me to stand and walk tall.

77. Daughter of the Lord
(For Emelda)

How great is he, I wonder
He isn't a Fai
Neither is he the Chairman
But e is Lord
The Lord of Hosts
He owns the world, all alone
And all the people therein are his oyster.

Are we his canon fodder?
For always, He is nigh
He may very well not be our nearest pressman
But he perches on the fort
And daily receives a thousand and one toasts
All of them on one phone
Above all,he calls me his daughter.

78. God from another Angle
(For Emeli)

Oh! If I were God!
I would make this world all over again
I would remake it, recreate it
Turn all men into women
And all women into men
And then watch them play together.

I wouldn't feed them with any cod
No, but I would offer them gifts wrapped and stood in the rain
Never would I think any pastor unfit
For I don`t know how the Almighty made his stamen
So, how would I match his deeds letter for letter?

79. Those Of Comfort
(For Comfort herself)

What really must I do to be herd?
Must I shout from the rooftops
Or kneel before the most high altar?
Must I first of all pray?
Does it really matter?
What happens now that I have a gagged mouth
And bound feet?

Although I am Comfort and not Hird
I do know about top of the pops
And above all, my alma matter
In my life, I have counted more than a sun's ray
Without ever having to batter
This beauty you proclaim is not from the south
It was simply imported in the last fleet.

80. What the Virgin Mother Wants
(For Susan)

Beauty and brains, what a combination!Or don`t you think
so?
What grabs me most are the contour lines
The missed symmetry and skewed research findings
But not so much the holy water
Or the altar sacrament
Or even the holy rosary.

Aren`t we all products of the great transfiguration?
Even if some of us came in with half a toe?

Nonetheless, we grow our own wines
And bear our own good tidings
Isn`t this also about smartness and the holy Father?
What we don`t want is another peppermint
So that even I, Susan, can boast of a second rosary.

81. A Problem and a Half

We have a problem
Though not about the Marxist slogans
Nor Mobutu`s tin of sour baked beans
No,it`s the meagre and chloroformed Yiddish contribution.

I may not be a second Moslem
Nor a former user of Morgan`s
But I know about all the virgin teams
And the great day of retribution.

82. Sprouts No One Wants

We`re behind the bars
For daring to spell our names backwards
Cryptic sprouts and moronic administrators
All of them with wet noses
Stood up like sheppardless sheep
And without shame
Testified against the Man of God.

83.Jokers From East London

They are all sick Jokers
That's what they are
They stink and groan
So don't give them a penny.

These guys shoot at anything that moves
And munch sprouted shrimps like starved brides
They gulp down leaven milk like castrated bullocks
The fools do that all day long
As if there was no tomorrow.

84. Bullets in Lipstick

How shall you count them?
How on earth shall we do it?
Crossed cannibals, gored palace chickens
And chained toothless bulldogs
That`s what they are
With their shallow buttocks
Sunken jaws and false teeth
Do you think they`ll hear you?

Why do you waste your gun powder?
Keep it in check
Save it for the rainy day
Above all
Save your breath for your porridge
If you have no underwear
Fetch the golden bible
Otherwise, you`re doomed.

51

85. Sentence Before Trial

The last man was out
So there was no need to venture in
Only the lame wishes of the bride
Or at the very least
The stained necklace of the pastor`s wife
Could dare the marooned king
And put a foot forward
That was why when the last of the Kaisers
Bellowed and camouflaged like a Bafang pig
Everyone quickly dug up their Nagasaki pearls and vanished.

86. Sugar Cane For Ever

We`ve taken care of it
We`ve sent it back, haven`t we Michele
So, let`s keep moving on
And for God`s sake
Let`s publish or perish.

If you think sugar cane is a hit
Just ask Michele
Not for fun
Or as a new form of rake
But a magic wand to cherish.

87. The Dusty Message

Let them,all of them, know it
Tell it them
But for God`s sake
Don`t bell them
In case they ask you to start knitting.

88. A Dime at Liverpool Street

I saw the cat game
It was certainly not for the lame
But it grew out of something eerie
And the odd Liverpool Street name,Cleary.

89. Kids' Questions About God

She`s my friend
That`s what Stanley said
About Lizzy
Because she accepted
To play with him
Stanley may not be Hogbe Nlend
Nor the Emir`s Fakir
But he`s Lizzy`s best Boh
See them play together
And Stanley asking her:
"Do you think it`s God?"

90. The South-Bound Vessel

No, I won`t board the sinking ship
Not again
Once bitten, twice shy
And that`s where I stand
Even if I stand alone.

Enough of Southampton
Why on earth must I vomit twice
On the same spot?
Nay, let`s swing around and head straight for the north
They won`t get us, even if they give chase
I`m not ready yet.

91. Archbishop Tutu's White Wings
(For Thembazaki Eunice Williams of Zambia)

South African angels have white wings
All of them
Although not all white wings in Pretoria belong to angels
That`s what the Holy Book says, to those who can read it.

If this world of ours were made of only little things
Wouldn`t we all love to touch and dearly cuddle them
Even if Durban preferred to bask all day long in the living
light?
Remember the archbishop says hard work keeps you fit?

92. Waiting for the Wanton Birds

I though I gave you one
Or am I dreaming?
Why would I, when the swan birds haven`t flown past?
Neither has the minister`s heart beat risen?

What we need most in Christendom is a crown
For God`s sake, not another farthing!
Lest the boss flies the flag at half mast
So let`s rejoice for Christ has risen.

93. So Much Waste Land

Did you use a citation
Or did you just cut and paste?
So when it`s time for confession
What shall you say about all the haste?

94. Alone with the Priest

I don`t like ammunition
Although I love cannons
But if I hear loose cannons
Then I rush to the priest for contrition.

95. Standing Betrayed

I have stood out here long enough
Every passing clown has noticed me, poor me
Splashed with pig`s blood
But I alone dry the tears of this nation
Oh! dream of the forgotten founding fathers!
Was this your wish?

96. Missing In Transit

I don`t know if it`s here
But I know it was sent
So, check again and have no fear
If you can`t find it, the caretaker must repent.

97. Global Sentence

Lecturers didn`t
Only students did
So when we came to the Cape of Good Hope
Everyone was accused of dope.

98. The Veil of Shame

Our golden seat is wet
So how on earth can we reserve it for her?
If she comes and causes a stir
Who shall rise and pull off the veil?

99. The Path Ahead

It isn`t normal at all
No, forget the packed launches
Pick up your holy bible and walk tall
That`s the only way you can avoid the trenches.

100. Awkward Act

All the birds have flown
Flown even before the Fon has sneezed
Flown before the young have grown
So, how shall the lone widows be quizzed?

101. The Parliamentary Mace
(For Dr. Joel Fusi Na`a Mukong)

I saw it
I saw it all
I saw it coming
I saw it with my own eyes
So, don`t start telling me stories.

Forget the pounding rain
Or the merciless floods
What matters is the mace
The one the governor`s man grabbed
And wreaked havoc in the National Assembly.

102. The Fifth Dose

Surely, a sledgehammer isn`t enough
We need God`s eternal wheelbarrow, and to boot, his will
So that once we wind the wind mill
All table birds will be rid of their cough.

103. Return Match

I will strike back
And match him dollar for dollar
We use the dollar
His ugly wings must be clipped
For too long
The idiot has dictated the pace
So, finally, who are we if not
Toothless dogs
And Lame ducks?

104. Forward March

He carried his luggage away
And strode like a peacock
No one could force him back into the shell
Because all previous promises had been broken.

105. Miracle Time

We may be blackened by centuries of bondage
But when the husbandmen arrive
All the floodgates will close up
The lame will walk
The deaf will hear
The blind will see
And the dumb will talk.

106. On That Day
(For Njeke Ngwa)

Shall these glories ever light up again?
Or shall they like the Titanic, go down for ever?
When all,that glitters ceases to be gold
Then shall we the down and out rise and walk.

107. The Wrong Frames

Don`t write epitaphs
They can never be monuments
Etch effigies on
http://www.blogger.com/img/blank.gifcanvass
No one will call you an ass.

108. Double Blessing

Our guilt is crystal clear
Conceived in vampiric jerks
But fashioned out of holy perks
What else can we hold on to with so much gear?

109. Still the Bible

The wooden bicycle isn`t enough
We must add a pinch of salt
Even if the bike is cluttered and disfigured
It is still the bible.

110. My Assigned Task

I wasn`t an idiot
Although everyone thought I was
I was the standard bearer
That`s why OI darn socks for auction.

111. Depressed Market Prices

It`s like conscience
Not omniscience
So when the sand pits overflow
Let not the victims soar.

112. Mouth of the Queen

Let the mouths speak
Let them all speak
But give them no vinaigrette
In case verbal strokes
All the way from Newcastle
Whet the queen`s dampened appetite.

113. My Holy Order
(For Njie Enow-Ebai-Enow)

I am a triumpher
Today celebrating my birthday
With the sun in Aquarius
My oysters are my pearls and my rubies
And my island; my bosom

The day I become an artful interpreter
Like old Jairius
I`ll fetch my crowns and my candies
And take off before the flowers blossom.

114. Love as a Wrapped Gift
(For Juliet Efuka Veseke)

Good, it feels to have a taste of true love
And I know what I`m on about
Even at midnight, forgotten nuns
All clad in their Sunday best
Stream out to commune with loved ones.

Today, at least, I`ve found my treasure trove
And I did so without a single bout
Nor any innings, nor runs
So if I`m put to the test
I`ll quickly offer my birthday cake to the blessed one.

115. Host from Fontem
(For Amindeh Blaise Atabong)

I am an ambidexter in every sense of the word
But I`m far from being your soldier hamster
What I need then
Is to be your five-star Lebialem host
That`s where I`ll celebrate my birthday.

116. Linear Progression
(For Sylvie Glenis Venyuy)

Growing old is compulsory
Growing up, optional
But when in good, old Baltimore
There's one thing I yearn for most
The dog that barked at me
When I thought of my birthday.

117. My Birthday as a Cock
(For Neba Diana Lum)

The desire to inspire and acquire, never to expire
That's my philosophy
For eulogies, homilies and frost bites
Forget pigs' furrows and dented hips
What counts is the talcumed hoof.

That's why in order to inspire
You must shun controversy
Even if you believe in the princess's rights
As such, when it comes to golden trips
My birthday will be the only cock under the roof.

118. All or Nothing
(For Tem Menging Honorine)

Every opportunity in life should not be spoiled
It should be grabbed as if it was the last
And made maximum use of
Life is like the wind
It blows in different directions at different times
Seize it now or lose it for ever
That`s it
There are no half measures
No midddle way
It`s all or nothing.
Happy birthday!

119. Life's Multiple Facets
(For Chia)

My life is exactly where it`s supposed to be
Upfront and centre-stage
I maintain a straight course
Head erect
Shoulders high
Not late
Not early
Just spot on
On the dot.

You may call me the Queen Bee
But, please, the one without rage
But when necessary, I can seek recourse
Like the President Elect

Who came hither and nigh
I don`t have a bait
Because I also want to be treated fairly
So that when my neighbour sues for fun
I`ll put her on the spot.

120. My Apostle`S Creed
(For Bei)

What I wish in life
Is all that I`ll include
In my letter to God the Almighty
I`ll ask him for good health in deed
Not a life of luxury
I`ll ask him for wisdom
Not only beauty
About which I am flattered.

In a world where evil is rife
And people tend to be rude
I`m bent on leaning heavily
On whatever is his will. That`s my daily bid
I don`t want to arrive in a flurry
When it comes to the Lord`s kingdom
Here at U.B., though, I have a duty
And that is to shower my God with praises daily.

121. The Love That Never Was

We met them by the pool of the village stream
And at once we knew their pants were crimson-red
If I were alone, I mean all alone
I would have known what to do
But alas!
This life being what it is
I was not to be alone
And so it was I lost the chance of my life
To do what I knew best.

122. The Game of Princes

Princes
All of them
Are nothing but needleword
What they need most is the needle
For fear of playing second fiddle
Always they want to push off the bulwark.

123. Bait for a Toe

Shall he wait
Or shall he go?
And if we stepped on her toe
Would she then drop the bait?

124. Alone For Lunch

Why so few feeding bottles?
Is it because of the crunch?
And what if we short-circuited all the throttles?
Would the First Lady then turn up for lunch?

125. Lost in the Jungle

In the midst of the down and out
I saw my face
Like the ghost face of Jackson
It was the living among the dead
Searching
Trudging
Shuffling
Disfigured
Changed
Transformed
Metamorphosized
Smelling
Unwanted
And dumped.

126. The Right Way

Don`t hold it that way
Hold it this way
Because if she makes another claim
We`ll all go lame.

127. The Spear From On High

What did they say?
That all spears must come down?
But how about the risen one?
Has he come down?

128. Rome as the Ultimate Price

What is the reason
If not treason?
And you say they deserve the bagpipes?
You may as well cede them Rome.

129. A Choir Too Many

Are you a hero or a mirror?
Famished, bruised and bleeding
You still sing praises
So what about the future generations?

130. The Vicious Circle

Let`s break this circle
And get out of here
Or do we want to go on limping
As if we were punished for the world`s sins?

131. Hankies as Last Flags

A million mouths for one loaf?
Only here in this country
And despite the buzzing flies
And the stained white hankies.

132. The Taboo Word

I can not pronounce the word
It`s too obscene
But if you want us to create a scene
Then I`ll say it`s the third.

133. The Royal Recipe

It`s not cognac
Neither is it a Big Mac
It`s water fufu and eru
Topped up with kata and fufu corn.

134. The Pastor`S Girl

She spoke the unspeakable
And got away with it
Just because
The pastor admired her voice.
That was it.

135. Victims of Prostitution

Prostitutes are risk takers
But not everyone is one
That`s why the one-day thief
Can easily get caught
And then is maimed for life.

136. The Painter's Hands

They were big hands
Not stained glass windows
If Michael Angelo were to return
We would burn a lot of midnight oil.

137. Voices from Yonder

We`re opening up
Not closing in
When a girl works too hard
She begins to hear voices.

138. City Lights Again

I`m on the high seas
All alone
But I`m not complaining
I`m simply telling it as it is.

When the glinting lid comes off
And the odalisque babes go missing
We shall all regret
We didn`t comb the city first.

139. Measurements for Two

It wasn`t the henchman
No, it was the footman
His measurements are taken in centimeters
Not millimeters.

140. Devices for the Monarch

The mechanism is alive
Just send a tinderbox for five
So that when the inevitable happens
We`ll know why the Queen Bee got rattled.

141. Stuff for the Loo

I didn`t deceive you
You refused to receive me
Just because I`m numb in the knee
It doesn't`t mean I was meant for you.

142. The Hidden Truth

Patricia has written
I received it this morning
But the letter came in ashes
My own letters burnt and the dust gathered up
As proof of my infidelity
If only she knew the truth!

143. My Location

I`m in the middle room
Not the prime minister`s lodge
In my right hand I carry a broom
But I bear no grudge.

144. The Road to Scoan

I want to follow him
All the way to SCOAN
If the prophet shows the way
Then the whole nation will rise and believe.

145. A Rope for Hope

He gives hope
And asks for nothing in return
When it comes to our turn
We ask for the rope.

146. The Last Ploughman and His Wife

The plowman is her
He came with his wife
To search for the meaning of life
So why be filled with rage and fear?

147. Letter for a Fool

This is my open letter
Dug up from the corner pool
If I weren`t a fool
I would have acted better.

148. Dogs of Change

We dread martyrdom
But we want change
If only we were dogs of war
We would have moved mountains.

149. Faith as One

Give them another chance
Please, don`t shoot them down
They`re the ones of faith
And we, the faint hearted.

150. Prayer Beads without a Round

It`s a good idea
One that will weigh more than a pound
But if they challenge us to a round
We won`t rise without asking for a beer.

151. Bout of the Day

She worked all day
Taking the rubbish bags out
But when we asked him to pray
She claimed we had declared another bout.

151. Suitor for Trish

What was it, really?
Just rat infested rubbish?
Then why did you get up so early
If not only to woo Trish?

152. Catalysts for Wives

He knows his fate
So save your breath for your porridge
The day we become hoofed ring leaders
Our wives will all run to the shopkeepers.

153. Scarecrow with a hoe

It was his word against ours
Forget about the maimed scarecrow
That`s why when mother sent for her hoe
We knew we`d starve for hours.

154. Hearing among Oars
(For all sons and daughters of Bota Island)

The oars are all roaring
Like the angry waves of Bota Island
When fishermen start to band
Who`ll seek the red herring?

155. Naked Truth

Could you say that to her face
Or would you only whisper it under your breath
Claiming that all jumpers of lace
Are both deep in starch and width?

156. The Standard Wretch

If I`m a wretch
You`re a drunkard
But at least, I don`t work for the Standard
And I know about the Treaty of Utretch.

157. Group Action

Like glue we`ll stick together
Tomorrow or the day after
Not in dad`s shirt sleeves
Or the headmistress`s borrowed robes
We`ll be clad in our wardrobe garments
Those the parish priest left after his retreat.

158. Men Who Act

We don`t ask questions
We simply act
Call us Yes Men or stooges
It won`t change anything.

159. The Gap Between

The gap is too large
Larger than life
Like New York, the big apple
But then where is the Stature if Liberty?

160. The Queen's Return

He sped past
As if rushing to Heathrow
Aghast,
The archbishop asked if the queen was back.

161. The Bottom Line
(For Eddie Momoh)

He gives what he has
The buzz, acid rain and animals
She gives what she hasn`t
Love, perfumed hankies and velvet toys.

162. Parents' Coloured Hands

Mother`s left hand is green
Her right hand, pink
Father`s right hand is pink
His left hand, green.

163. Crossing Branches

My tree branches won`t cross
So, don`t bother
Put back your axes
And pick up your wheelbarrow.

164. Cows in Stockwell

I know cows well
I've lived with them
Not in Bethlehem
But in good, old Stockwell.

165. My Fright of Hills

I really don't like hills
They pose like bully boulders
With large gaps between their teeth
And Frost's yelping dogs
Too thirsty for blood to retreat.

166. The Price of a Secret

I know the secret
And I'll tell you if you give me
A female wasp, a cup of black coffee
A calabash of overnight palm wine
Two male goats
A mature white cock
Seven six-lobe cola nuts
An unopened tin of palm of
And the sum of a million Francs.

167. The Lawless State

I don`t like sponges
They`ve soaked everything I have
Where then is equity?
Where's the legislative arm?

168. Judas in the Family

My heart is in distress
She left me this morning
Carting away my wedding ring and bible
She eloped with my best man.

169. Born Again

It`s all futile
So give it up
Think nothing of luxury
Give your life to Christ.

170. High Society Party

When it comes
We shall be there
Even without our apples
We shall be given access.

171. She as Sole Proprietor

I`m done with you
You`re not my Cancerian RAK
So why ask me for the world?
All I possess is hers.

172. Life as a Peacock

Life is never straight
It comes in contours and meanders
If you`re not thehttp://www.blogger.com/img/blank.gif
wooden man
You won`t even
remembehttp://www.blogger.com/img/blank.gifr the first
verse.

173. Deceptive Colours

Colours can really be misleading
They make you miss your step
But turn out to be only a mirage
Far off hills looking green.

174. Night Duty

He massaged his head
All night
Outside, the owls suffocated
All night.

175. The Cursed One

These whispering birds aren`t cursed
We are
That`s why we pray daily
And they feast daily.

176. Pop Up At the Pool

I didn`t see him drown
In the municipal lake
But I was told
I saw his fly-infested clothes by the pool
And like they predicted
On the third day
His body surfaced on the pool.

177. The First Lady's Nipples

I didn`t count her nipples
But I noticed they were legion
And they were crowded like cattle in a pen
It`s not only runaway nuns called Rose Kate
Whose nipples have something to write home about.

178. The End Loser

In the end
I who stood still
Have become the loser
Yet, I`m neither the revenge seeker
Nor the muscle developer
Nor the railway signal man
Nor the court registrar
Nor the Council ombudsman.

179. Bethroted to a Prince

That`s my last hope
That she comes back
Not with the golden fleece
But with the charming prince.

180. On Self Exile
(For Ngafor Antoine. He and I know best the man who should have left without a forwarding address)

I will rise and speak
When everyone else is silent
And I will tell the truth
The whole truth
Let no one stop me
Not even my parish priest
Because after the rally
I`m taking off
I will go never to return

And without leaving a forwarding address.

181. Drunk with Love

I can feel her touch
It`s as sweet as honey
Her angelic breath; yes - that one
Lifts me above all heights
Today I`m simply drunk with love.

182. The Truth about Stone Walls

Stone walls don`t speak
But they`re choking with words
That`s why from the Stature of Liberty
Any wall looks like a stone wall.

183. The End of Sweetness

Sweetness is nothing
Not even a winged bird
But if your holed up in an iron cage
You`ll think the end is near.

184. Thirst as a Sphynx

Thirst isn`t grief
Far from it, it`s an appetizer
So when you smell fermented corn beer
Don`t yet sing your last hymn.

185. A Dollar for Obama

One dollar isn`t enough
Make it two
Do you think it`s that easy
To push a confidential note to Obama
While he presides over a cabinet meeting?

186. Angst of the Gods

The gods are angry
And our forefathers jittery
If we in turn become so watery
Then how shall the village solve the quandary?

187. Love For Two

When love comes down
With wings at last unclipped
The lone damsel will float in a gown.
But let no Kom man be irked.

188. Marooned on an Island

Oh! Rose of my life!
Where is your gloss?Or is it your cross?
I`m stuck here in Fyffe.

189. Singing for the Dead

You must stand up and sing
If you want to be remembered
But if your notes are too long for meaning
Then the old matron`s bones must be deterred.

190. The Stray Researcher

Where does he think he is going
Carrying Gertrude`s prized wedding photograph?
Is he banking on quantitative analysis
Or is he thinking of the quantitative approach?
Check it out.

191. THE PRESIDENT`S SPEECH

The president`s speech was subtle
But it wasn`t Isaac Newton
He had all the right articulations
And spelt out all the right policies
But who was listening?

192. In Bed with Awan Angob's Cat

This is Awan`s cat
The new one with sparkling eyes
Not the black one that got missing
Tonight I`ll climb on Awan`s plank bed
Call up the cat
And together we`ll pull up the old blanket
And play hide and seek
Then while Pussie purrs in her sleep
I will listen attentively
So that when Awan awakes
I`ll tell her everything.

193. Lessons from Paris

I like the silver runways of Paris
They are like Paradise on earth
Liberty, Equality and Fraternity
That`s what it`s all about
When shall we ever learn?

194. Danger of the Gusts

Many have said it before
So, I`m not reinventing the wheel
When the great gusts rise
Tye`ll bring down everything
Even the sky.

195. Three Quick Steps

The steps are steep
Like those of the White House
But if we`re snappy
We`ll beat them to it.

196. The Joker and the Ear

The ear doesn`t hear any longer
Even when it goes to school
But if you call it a fool
It labels you a miserable joker.

197. Common Enemies

My enemies are back
And back in force
Were not we all black
I would have sought recourse.

198. The One On Trial

The glare was forbidding
That`s why she squinted
Anyone who accuses her of fondling
Must first prove he hasn`t deserted.

199. No Floor for Sea Monsters

The sea monsters are back
And back with a vengeance
When the delayed ship sails in
No crew member will have the floor.

200. Striking a Balance

Golden lamps aren`t really what we want
Send us bags of rice and salt
It`s not nickel or cobalt
Just what is remaining of the old grant.

201. Tears That Do Not Drop

Tears aren`t good
Despite what the priest says
But if you think they`re food
Then ferry them us in trays.

202. Salvation for a Few

This is the day the Lord has appointed
Nothing slippery or winged shall walk
Only beleaguered mothers down with the flu
Shall travel the whole length
All alone.

203. Odd Messages from Arabia

My old man spoke first
But his speech was a heap of stones
The the Holy One coughed
And his cough was perfumed air from Arabia.

204. The Sunday Reader

She came on a Sunday
And read from Luke
Although she said she was no crook
I knew we`d prove her wrong some day.

205. Shelves of Dough

We have enough
For our boys and ourselves
So just look on the shelves
And send me some dough.

206. In Search of the Campass

I stood before the brook
Like some new Douala crook
Surely, if I wasn`t rude
I would soon again be en route.

207. Steady on the Path

I wasn`t in wrath
I wasn`t even upset
I was only seeking the path
Before the much vaunted sunset.

208. The Palm Of God`S Servant

His palms are moist
Like those of Mr Davidson
Where then is the Lord`s relic
If not once more buried in relics?

209. The Code of Conduct

Watch when I speak
And listen when I yawn
Across the bridge
The good Lord will unfailingly take note.

210. The Nation We Set Ablaze

I sincerely think that we erred
We didn`t break the sword, yes
But we fanned the flames
That`s why the nation is on fire.

211. The Pilot, the Vice Chancellor and I

When I put up my hand
The pilot looks away
When I then cross the bar
The Vice Chancellor giggles.

212. Why We Love

Mbonshu, you wonder why we love at all
We love
We all do, don`t we?
Because we feel insecure
And unfulfilled
Because we`re messed up.

So like the round ball
We seek a partner, a treasure trove
Whether on land or at sea
And call it our own property and tenure
It doesn`t matter whether it was willed or unwilled
We just want a top up, another top up.

213. The Final Number

I have run the race
And fought the good fight
Today I`m at my tether`s end
The die is cast
And the curtains, drawn.

But like Gbagbo, I`ll go at my own pace
Because I know my right
I have no more fences to mend
I know the Lord`s kingdom is vast
The only thing I want right now is another prawn.

214. Unlike A Sapele

Don`t mistake me for a sapele
A sapele is a plant
But I`m not
I think and feel and act
And I have dominion
Before me the sapele is nothing
It`s speechless
Powerless
Impotent
So how do you liken me to it?

215. Here to Serve

We`re all God`s handmaids
Not drowning men
Or worse still, dying horses
We`re willing guinea pigs
And the last able-bodied seamen.

216. Blowing Hot and Cold

If it`s really hot, well, blow it
If it`s still hot, try oiling it
If that fails, send for the archbishop in person
He`ll bring his Sunday missal.

217. Landresses on Sunday
(For Gideon Kweti)

Don`t pile on the strawberries
They`re bitter enough already
Instead, do egg on the laundresses
They`re ready and raring to go.

But for God`s sake, don`t come in lorries
Lest everyone thinks we`re heady
Instead, come resplendent in your Sunday best dresses
For once, forget about the hoe.

218. The Swapped Roles

While with Sakwe and Tomdio I lit candles at the sacristy
She sold groundnuts and akra to the workers
She did so, even more than the preacher
Believing she was fighting human adversity.

219. Goods of Burden

We didn`t send them back
So don`t hold us to it
How could we
When we didn`t have the secret code?

220. Lilies as Day and Night

Lilies aren`t all the dame
Just as tulips too differ
They all have joints, yes
But their receptacles point in different directions
That`s why one is day
And the other, night.

221. The Run Away River

The river ran along, alone, all alone
And not even the pastor could match it
Flat-bottomed prostitutes brought wheel barrows
And saber-rattling men cried out for blood
As if they were another Bismark
The Iron Chancellor
So why didn`t they stop the river?

222. Paced Footsteps

I`m not in a hurry
I`ve slowed down
Unless you think me a clown
Whom you`re out to bury.

223. How to Do it

How do they do this thing?
How on earth do they do it?
Do they start by tattooing
And then fill up and top up
With ginger from Ngaoundere?

I don`t get it
Despite my vision
And what they showed me
Does that mean
The macrocosm is lower than the microcosm
And the shoulders higher than the head?

224. The President's Visit

No birds chirped
No serpents hissed
No toads croaked
No horses brayed.

But everyone including the Commissioner
Clamored for a garland
Then an empty altar bowl
And cowrie beads without the dames
All of that
Just to make the loudest noise for the president.

225. Hibiscus for the Bees

I see a hibiscus flower
Taller than the pope`s tower
But if the mask is pulled off
The fertile bees will fly off.

226. A Bowl of Love
(*For my one and only Emilia*)

Oh, sweet glory
What can irk you so?
Why do you cough?
Why do you sneeze?
Come to me this instant
And I`ll give you rest
Peace

Attention
Affection And above all, love.

227. Bait for Trisha

The horror is over
So tell Trisha to return
Our treasures are once more visible
And the orchard branches, resplendent
What more does she want?

228. The Green Card

Out of this country
I`m nobody
That`s why I won`t trade my soul
For Uncle Sam`s card.

My umbilical chord is interred here
So are my ancestors
Above all, my future is rooted here
Even if I fly out, I must still fly in
Some day.

229. Sunday in Bombay

Did you say, Bombay
Or Sunday?
Whatever it was
Fetch my umbrella
My scarlet scarf
And my wind cheater
And tell the prince I`m on my way.

230. The Sound of Silence

If we`re here today, boys
It`s for the sake of the parish priest
And not the best man`s toys
So if you have your cell phones with you
Please, put them off.

231. Long Live the Queen

I had Kenyan tea
And the river bank
A handful of warriors
And out I went
To greet the newly crowned queen.

232. A Rabbit on the Run

Look at that one
Just look at it
With his rabbit ears
He`ll soon shed tears.

He thinks he owns the road
But he doesn`t know he`s just a toad
If you declare him null and void
He`ll instead think he`s buoyed.

279. Chickens Too Good For Christmas

Have the chickens not come home?
Don`t they know it`s Christmas today?
Or do they simply take us for new gnomes
And our kindred for wrapped gifts for the Lamas?

280. God, the Greatest

Wake me Lord, when I`m asleep
Feed me Lord, when I`m hungry
Pour down the drink Lord, when I`m thirsty
Give me hearing Lord, when I`m dumb
Give me sight Lord, when I`m blind
Whisk me away, Lord when I`m tempted
Turn me around Lord, when I turn away.

Make me your slave Lord, when I disown you
Gag my mouth Lord, when I curse you

Tie my legs Lord, when I walk away from you
Tag me Lord, when I confuse you
Smack me Lord, when I don`t worship you
Flatten me like bread flour on the table, oh Lord
If I question you.

For who am I , if not your wanton sheep?
Who am I if not your holy temple?
What am I if not an unworthy child?
What am I if not a mere parasite?
I am nothing but trouble to you?
What is my future without you, if not a bleak one?

That`s why when I`m downcast, you cheer me up
When I`m weak at the knees, you carry me
When I sneeze, you pat me on the back
When I weep, you wipe my tears.
Who else is greater than thou
Who on this whole wide earth?
Nobody
None
Only you
Because you are the greatest.

281. The Lord as My Fortress

Not only does my own soul sing
It pines for the Lord
When I`m wounded and afflicted
And have no more straw to draw
I turn to him for comfort and solace
He is my rock, by barricade, my fortress and my refuge.
He is my life, my future and my destiny.

282. Logs Too Short for the Lord

Will these few logs do?
Or shall we again send for the handyman?
If we don`t want another boo
Let`s plot and execute like the last journeyman.

283. The Egg Men from Meiganga

We`re all egg men
Even you
So don`t start blowing hot and cold
That won`t get you anywhere.

We`re not in Meiganga because we like it
Meiganga was forced on us by the wind
You see? The wind again
So beware of egg men.

284. The Weight of Bricks

The charge is high, too high
If a single brick weighs a ton
Then what would we expect of the cross
If it wasn`t carried by our Lord?

285. A Holow Sham

Yes, I will say it again
I will even shout it if you want
This blackened roof top of a sanctuary
Is the worst hollow sham I`ve even seen
Go and tell the governor
If you like.

286. The Palm Of God's Servant

His palms are moist
Like those of Mr Davidson
Where then is the Lord`s relic
If not once more buried in relics?

287. Today's Impress
(For George Njwe, MBUDCA President, Buea Branch)

Your is a cut above the rest
That`s why it`s the best
But when you reach the crest
It will be at my behest.

288. Alone With the Same House that Jack Built
(Reminiscences of an old nursery school rime that left a lasting impression on me).

I saw the house that Jack built
I saw it with my own eyes
But I found no rat in it
However, I found scattered grains of corn
Strewn all over the floor
As if the rats had just visited
Apart from that odd find
Nothing else lay in the house that Jack built
So I wondered
Should I trek all the way to Nottingham
To see what legacy Lord Byron left
Or should I contend myself with
The leftovers of the sour malt
And the loose white hairs from the beleaguered cat`s body
The footman said he preserved?
And why should I believe him anyway?
I didn`t see the dog, nor the man, nor the priest nor the
maiden
But as I came away disappointed
I heard ringing in my poor ears
Children`s deafening voices singing
This is the house that Jack built.

289. Grandma's Knee

One more sound
Just one more
And you`re dead
You can trust me.

If God`s world wasn`t round
And all axe men weren`t one
Then everything on this earth would I dread
Even grandma`s knee.

290. The Queen's Thing

It`s not a stereotype
Neither is it media hype
It`s something stolen from Halloween
Just for the queen
My queen.

292. Splashes of A Father's Coffee
By Tikum Mbah Azonga

Coffee also blooms and blossoms
When it`s time
That`s what my dad told me
And that`s what I saw.

If you live in the upper rooms
And each day imbibe a drop of lime
You`ll also prefer coffee to teat
And you`ll detest cubes of ice that refuse to thaw.

293. Gods Raft of Certainty
(For Mola Charles Menyoli)

I will shower your name with blessings
And cover your path with flowers and perfume
I will ask all the chirping birds of Gods air
To fetch their golden harps in wait
And all Mile 17 Park Boys with their strident voices
To converge like one man at the motor park
And with one voice, proclaim your holy name
You are God, you are Lord, and you are the most high.

I won't forget Fakoship`s stevedorings
Because I don't want you to fume
And also because to Mola Menyoli I must be fair
With God, Fakoship will not lapse
For he alone will forestall all its vices
And never will he let anyone be another Clark
Lord, yesterday, today and tomorrow, you are same

Our only wish is to be nigh and high.

FOOTNOTE

I wrote this poem on New Year`s eve, that is the 31st of December 2009 while dining at LADY L Restaurant in Limbe. Suddenly I thought about Pa Mola Charles Menyoli, the boss of FAKOSHIP, with whom I hadn`t met for about five years. Interestingly, a few minutes after I finished writing the poem and was still sitting at LADY L, I saw him pass in his vehicle. This was remarkable, I thought. Why see him only when I had just written a poem for him?

Pa Menyoli is one of the Cameroonians whom I hold in very high esteem. He once gave me a rousing reception at his Buea residence some ten years ago when I was on a mission in Cameroon from Britain which at the time, was my base. Apart from that, Mola Menyoli is a man with a kind heart. He is done a lot in terms of giving something back to the community. Those who know him, know that about him.

294. Change at the Top

You talk of change?
What change?
Change of the guard
Or change at the top?
Has the bottom not fallen out
Like some old wine in new wine skins ?
Or new wines in old wine skins?
Aren't we just going round in circles?

After so many years of change
It's back to Square One at full range
If you doubt me, ask the coast guard
All he has is champagne to pop
Every male has been subdued by the political rout
Children with distended stomachs live like urchins
Heaped on them and their mothers are our leaders` sins
All fish have lost their left ventricles.

295. The Left Handed Child

I am a left hander and I admit it
Freely, democratically and willingly
Without coercion or duress or peer pressure
I didn't beg for it, neither did I buy it
God made it so and he knows why
In his infinite wisdom.

But what haven't I suffered from mankind
Insults, beatings, torture, persecution and execution
For no crime other than that I used what God gave
Who is man to question God?
How can a root question the top of the tree?

295. God's Foundation Stone

God is a God of love
He is a good God
He is the light that shineth
For those buried in the depths of despair
And the abyss of condemnation.

Through his love
And in his name as God
Even the voiceless and the sightless from Elizabeth
Can still rise and shine with greatest repair
We call that, laying the foundation.

296. My Book of Psalms
(For Emmanuel of the PCC Synod Office, Buea)

I have talked about kindness
But not secrecy
I have written about freedom
But not neglect
I have read about husbandmen
But not sour vineyards.

Today the virtue I seek most to harness
Is walking in the footsteps of the Lord`s advocacy
Because what I seek is his kingdom
As an education staff, he to me is the only one to elect
Because he died for all men
So, why can`t we be his life guards?

297. Storm in a Tea Cup

I'm not hiding
No! Why would I?
I have nothing to hide
Absolutely no skeletons in the cupboard
I'm the open book
That can be read by anybody.

If you started off on the wrong foot
Please, don't take it out on me
I'm not the Urban Council
Let alone Hysacam
Too many bird droppings in my backyard already
So how can I start hatching new eggs now?

298. God's Living Sign
(For Claudia)

What a blessing, in deed!
On this blessed day of our Lord
I call this a miracle from above
This day on which the white turtle
Perched on my little head
Like the apostles` tongue of fire.

I know the apostles` creed
Even without riding a ford
So, when Sister Irene thinks I have a stock
I tell her: "No, *Grande Soeur*, it`s only the throttle."
For have I suddenly become some lad
Or a cheap hand for hire?

299. The Task At Hand
(For Uncle Peter Esoka)

You can get it
Yet, you can take it out right now
If you really want
But first, let Peter come through
And deliver today`s dlose of reflection
Peter and us are now like finger and nail
With maleya in the background
And the tune that made them
Shoot to fame spectacularly
What more can you ask for?

Meanwhile, Ecobank is celebrating proximity

And the weighing bridge is announced
Jumping little girls and boys in green
Stoop along the road
And write their names in the shifting sand
And yellow petrol l procession
Is that what you want?
Just that?
And you think you`ve had your fair share
When you can go the whole way
And pick up the jackpot
Come on!
You can get it
If you believe you can.

300. Off On a Limb

I`m out at last
Out in this whole wide world
And walking tall and free
And taunting the wanton lilies.

If it wasn`t for the haunted flag
I would have gone out again
Like Maye Sunsaye
Just to test the celebrity waters.

301. The Long Wait

I have waited long enough
In fact for too long
Far too long
The last birds have flown
And the flags are at half mast.

Life here is very tough
And nowhere
Nowhere do I hear a love song
Only the hapless age-old gong
If I knew my baby had grown
Would I still be an outcast?

302. Why I Run

I hear a voice
It is loose and unleashed
Yesterday it was muffled and gagged
Today, it`s a shadow of its old self.

I want to make a choice
To show the world I`m unabashed
That even if I`m tagged
I can`t be exposed on the shelf.

303. My Last Stance

For God`s sake,what does that mean?
Shall we for ever walk backwards
One step forward, two steps backward?
Or shall we, for once just jump?

I may not be the best father
But I honestly hope I`m not awkward
Although I may look lime a coward
Nowhere on me can you find a lump.

304. One Way Ticket

She hasn`t returned
She hasn`t even written
I`m now surprised
Becaause she left with only her handbag.

She asked for the tray that was burned
In order to spite her kitten
But today, look how her teeth are priced
That`s why we brought out the sand bag.

305. Too Little, Too Late

Nobody comes closer now
Not even you
So stand back from the porch
And let the lead sink.

306. Missing Bone

I know a bone when I see one
And I mean every word of that
That`s why when I sniff at a cone
I rush for my fur hat.

307. My Solemn Right

I have the right to sneeze
But what I won`t do is freeze
But if my joystick sinks
Then I`ll put on my cuff links.

308. The Toothless Dog

I must strike a balance
And by all means, not later than today
Go and tell him that
Tell him to stop his slander
I have been there before
I have seen it all before
So let him silence that his choir
Let him stop behaving like a lout
Let him come clean and cut.

For a yes or a no
That man would sell his soul
Has he ever cared about anyone?
Let alone himself?
Even when I was at the bank

I heard his so-called sound bites
His velvet sights and sounds
But I tell you what?
He is nothing buy a toothless dog.

309. A Bridge Too Far

This is the Dreamland girl`s sister
She knows all about pudding at Easter
So if you think you`re the next bishop
Never again will the nuns come to shop.

310. Collect Call

Did you call for him
Or did he call for you?
Or am I barking up the wrong tree?
Would you mind telling me, Miss World?

311. Rebel with a Cause

I won't stand here and watch this
I refuse to be a party to it
I won't be an eye witness to man's inhumanity to man
Stand by while God's world spins on its axis
And while robust women with enough breast
Push sopping and rotten bits of bread without butter
Into the numb mouths of babies left for too long
Far too long out in the rain and cold?

I' m out of it even if you take me for a novice
Why should I - why on earth should I sit
Then get up and curse the tree as if I wasn't human?
What about the man with axes?
One must decide whether one's on the trough or the crest
Since I've been my own hunter
Rather than maim, I'll prolong
My greatest wish is to return to the fold.

312. The Football King
To all Shesans

I saw Song today
I don`t mean, Daniel
No, I`m talking about Rigobert
So, it`s not the journalist
It`s the footballer.
I saw the football king today
It was in Bassaland
His nativeland, where his navel was buried

Like that of Roger Milla
I saw him in Sanaga Maritime Division
Along the Yaounde-Douala highway
As we drove to Douala
Song was smiling broadly
From ear to ear
Beaming
On a roadside poster.
He wore his legendary dreadlocks
Like a man who had just been told
He had been admitted into heaven
With the privilege of getting there
Without having to die first
Yes, more or less like Tony Banks
When he learned Tony Blair
Leader of the just come back New Labour
Had appointed him Sports Minister.

You ask why I call Song Rigobert
`The Football King`
You want to know why not Eto`o
Or Milla
Or Pele
And you say if Song is good
I could call him something else
Not the King
Well, of all the above
Song is the tallest and the most stout and the most handsome
He looks like a swash buckling soldier
So he can defend you against any enemy
Even Idi Amin, if he were to return.

Song is a Foot king in his own right
If you`re still doubting
Remember that those others are kings
Only because they shone as part of a team.
Thrust into the football pitch alone
All, all alone
Like the lone mariner on the high seas
They would not play
There would be none to play with
And none to play against
Worse still, there would be no linesman
No referee
No match delegate
No spectator
So even as the greatest world kings
They would be null and void
Nought
Zero
Toothless dogs.
They would lose the match
And lose woefully
Not through forfeiture
But through an unscored lone goal.
And wouldn`t that be a shame!

313. The Name Game

I don`t know what to say
So, don`t ask me
All I know is he gave
He was here
He came and he left it.

Yes, that may not be your pay
But why ask me?
Don`t you know what`s in a name?
Anything, as long as it`s near
Unless you think it`s a bottomless pit.

314. Dancing Kings

It`s not a race
So, slow down
Hold your horses
There`s time for everything
Besides, by rushing
You can simply fudge things.

It`s not because you`re wearing lace
Let alone a frown
As long as you don`t join forces
Your life will be only a fling
No fishing, no musings, no wrenching
Just because you decided to grow wings.

315. My Share of the Cross

I have died a thousand deaths
Yet I live
What haven`t I gone through?
I`ve been through thick and thin
I`ve been insulted and reproached
Slandered, disqualified and ostracized
Spat on and humiliated.

Even so, I stand tall
And stand firm
I hold my ground
After all, what`s one fall?
Jesus fell, not once
Nor twice
But thrice.
So who am I to moan?

316. Nativity Time Fever

Christmas is here
And here with a bang
The streets here in Yaounde are jammed
And everyone is in a hurry
In a mad rush
It's a race
A rat race
Some kind of race for time
But isn't it just a few hundred kilometers to nowhere?

All the men dream of is beer
They tank it regardless of the big bang
That's why daily we're crammed
So we either unearth or we bury
The unlikely two will fight the thrush
Just because of this so-called modern craze
And just because everyone wants to save face
But then when the bells chime
Shall we remember that Christ is everywhere?

317. Eyeball-To-Eyeball

I don't like winged animals
They're too petty for me
They sniff at the wrong times
And snore when they don't have to
Their hair is always messy and disheveled
They are unkempt and unshaven
And carry about red roundish eyeballs in the wrong sockets
They do that all the time
That's why my parish priest at Bolifamba is fond of saying
The Lord is good all the time
All the time the Lord is good.

318. Man at the War Front

I left it in the virgin orchard
I did so myself
Not by proxy
Nor by remote control
I put it away personally
Out of harm's way
So that tomorrow
When my son grows up
And starts counting the colours of the rainbow
He can also stoop and conquer
And bring home all his men
Complete with their overalls and sweat shoes.

319. Not A Farthom More, Not A Farthom Less
(For Alice)

Am I sure?
Even for a farthing
I'd stand clear of them
And call a spade a spade
So, as you can see
I'm cock sure.

I'm not a crook
Crooks put the cart before the horse
And call it expertise
As if they were the World Bank.

No, I'm a gentleman
Gentlemen see a man going the wrong way
And at once put him back on the right track
Even if they have to accompany Alice to Wonderland.

320. Were You There?

Where you there when he hit the ground running
Or were you there only when he put his foot in his mouth?
Where you there when he got up and walked tall
Or were you there only when he shot himself in the foot?

So how can you, today of all days
Stand up and claim, sghgamelessly
It was you who caught his falling mango
And it was you who posted his love letter?